Also by Nigel Blundell in Piccolo
I Suppose You Think That's Funny?

THE BEASTLY JOKE BOOK

by Nigel Blundell
with Dee Blundell

Illustrations by David Woodward

A Piccolo Original
Piccolo Books

First published 1989 by Pan Books Ltd
Cavaye Place, London SW10 9PG
9 8 7 6 5 4 3 2 1
Text © Nigel Blundell, 1989
Illustrations © David Woodward
ISBN 0 330 30758 4

Printed and bound in Great Britain by
Richard Clay Ltd, Bungay, Suffolk

Introduction

The world of animals is a weird and wonderful place.

The chameleon can change colour. The snake can shed its skin. The worm can split in half and grow again.

We learn all that and more at school and on TV.

But what they don't tell us are some of the many more astonishing facts about the natural world. . .

Have you ever heard, for instance, why giraffes have such long necks? The answer, quite simply, is because they've got smelly feet.

You may think that hyenas are the only animals that laugh. In which case you can't have heard of that rare beast, the happy-potamus.

Teachers may tell us about the duck-billed platypus. But do they ever mention that strange duck-eating cat, known as the duck-filled fatty-puss?

With this book, you can fill in all those glaring gaps in your knowledge.

You will even be able to answer that hitherto imponderable question: Why do elephants paint the soles of their feet yellow?

The answer is, of course: so that they can't be seen when they hide upside down in a bowl of custard.

What's that you say. . . ? *You* have never found an elephant upside down in your custard?

Just proves it works, then – doesn't it!

What would you get if you crossed a watch dog with a werewolf?
Very nervous postmen.

Hear about the tiger who caught measles?
He became so spotty the other tigers banished him to the leopard colony.

Which animal never fights fair?
The cheetah.

What is the best way to talk to a roaring lion?
Long distance.

A lion cub was chasing a hunter round a tree.
Mother lion says: 'How many times have I told you not to play with your food'.

What do you get if you cross a hyena with a myna bird?
An animal that laughs at its own jokes.

Where would a zoo-keeper hang his washing?
On the clothes lion.

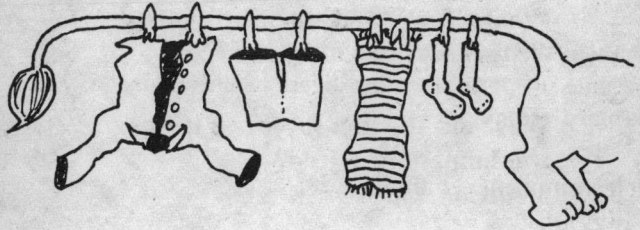

Why does a bear wear a fur coat?

Because he would look ridiculous in a mackintosh.

How do you start a bear race?
Ready, Teddy, Go!

What's furry and worn by nudists?
Bear skins.

What did the lion say when it saw two hunters in a jeep?
Meals on wheels.

Where do you find wild boar?
Depends where you leave them.

Fred: 'My dad's a big game hunter in London. . . He shoots lions.'
John: 'But there aren't any lions in London.'
Fred: 'Just proves he's a good hunter.'

Have you ever seen a man-eating tiger?
No, but I have seen a man eating chicken.

Mother to neighbour: 'I took little Jimmy to the zoo and he got into trouble.'
Neighbour: 'Why, what was he doing?'
Mother: 'He was feeding the monkeys.'
Neighbour: 'What's wrong with that?'
Mother: 'He was feeding them to the lions.'

There were two lions walking down Oxford Street.
One lion said to the other: 'Quiet here, isn't it?'

A couple on safari were walking through the jungle when suddenly a huge lion sprang out in front of them, seized the wife in its jaws and started to drag her off into the bush.

'Shoot!' she screamed to her husband. 'Shoot!'

'I can't,' he replied. 'I've run out of film!'

What did the grizzly bear take on holiday with him?
The bear essentials.

Why is a lion in the desert like Christmas?

Because of its Sandy Claws.

What is the difference between a wet day and a lion with toothache?
One is pouring with rain and the other is roaring with pain.

How many lions can you put in an empty cage?
One. After that the cage is not empty.

13

If there was a tiger on your right, a lion on your left, one elephant in front of you and one behind, what would you do?
Get off the merry-go-round.

What's furry and minty?
A Polo bear.

What do you get if you cross a lion with a parrot?
I don't know but if he says 'Pretty Polly', smile.

What do you call a deaf tiger?
Anything at all – he won't hear you.

Why can't leopards escape from the zoo?
Because they are always spotted.

What do you call a 100 kilo grizzly bear with a bad temper?
Sir.

A big-game hunter always boasted:
'I shoot 'em right between the eyes.'
He was eaten by two one-eyed tigers prowling together.

How can you come face-to-face with a hungry, angry lion and still walk away unharmed?
Walk to the next cage.

What's the difference between a coyote and a flea?
One howls on the prairie and the other prowls on the hairy.

What's the difference between the Prince of Wales and a daddy gorilla?
One is the heir apparent – the other is a hairy parent.

What is the best way to hunt bear?
With your clothes off.

Why are wolves like playing-cards?
They both come in packs.

What's grey, heavy and sends people to sleep?
A hypnopotamus.

What do baby apes sleep in?
Apricots.

'Would you rather a lion ate you or a gorilla?'
'I'd rather it ate the gorilla.'

What's the difference between a thought, a sigh, a mink coat, and a monkey?
A thought is an idea, a sigh is 'Oh dear!', a mink coat is too dear, and a monkey is you, dear.

How do you get a rhinoceros in a Mini?
Chuck one of the elephants out.

Two Africans were sitting on a bank of a river.
Suddenly, one let out a yell.
'What's the matter?' asked the other.
'A crocodile has just bitten off my foot.'
'Which one?'
'What does that matter? Those crocodiles all look alike to me.'

Why did the monkey put a slice of bread on his head?
'Cos he thought he was a grilla.

Which animal has the highest intelligence?
A giraffe.

What kind of monkey eats chips?
A chipmunk.

What's tall and smells nice?

A giraff-odil.

What's worse than a giraffe with a sore throat?
A centipede with fallen arches.

What do you get if you cross an apple with an alligator?
An apple that bites you before you can bite it.

What do you get if you cross a camera with a crocodile?
A snapshot.

If a crocodile makes shoes what does a banana make?
Slippers.

What do you get if you cross a crocodile with a rose?
I don't know, but I shouldn't try to smell it.

What's a crocodile's favourite game?
Snap.

Customer: 'I'd like a pair of crocodile shoes.'
Shop owner: 'Certainly, madam. What size does your crocodile take?'

Teacher: 'This afternoon I want to tell you all about the hippopotamus. Please pay attention, all of you! If you don't look at me you'll never know what a hippopotamus is like.'

Teacher: 'Where are rhinos found?'
Pupil: 'Please, miss, rhinos are so large they hardly ever get lost.'

Why does a hippopotamus have red toenails?
So that he can hide in a cherry tree.

What weighs two tonnes and has a flower behind its ear?

A hippypotamus.

How do you stop a rhino charging?
Take away its credit card.

What do you get if you cross a monkey with egg whites and sugar?
A meringue-utan.

How did the chimpanzee escape from his cage?
He used a monkey wrench.

What would you get if you crossed a giraffe with a hedgehog?
A long-handled brush.

What's worse than a giraffe with a sore throat?
An elephant with a nose bleed.

Teacher: 'What are the five animals in the giraffe family?'
Pupil: 'Mother Giraffe, Father Giraffe, and three baby giraffes.'

Why do giraffes have such long necks?

Because they can't stand the smell of their feet.

Which are the snootiest animals in the zoo?
Giraffes, because they look down on people.

Why does a giraffe need so little to eat?
Because it makes a little go a long way.

What is Dracula's favourite animal?
The giraffe – just think of all that neck!

What's worse than a giraffe with a sore throat?

A tortoise with claustrophobia

What do you get if you cross a monkey with a flower?
A chimp-pansy.

Knock, Knock.
Who's there?
Monkey.
Monkey who?
Monkey won't fit, that's why I knocked.

How do you get a one-armed monkey down from an orange tree?
Wave at him.

What's black, white and red and runs on sixteen wheels?
A sunburnt zebra on roller-skates.

What do you get if you cross a zebra with a pig?
Striped sausages.

What did the traffic lights say to the zebra crossing?
Don't look now – I'm changing.

What's black and white and stops buses?
A zebra crossing.

What is black, white and red all over?
An embarrassed zebra.

What's black and white and noisy?
A zebra with a drum-kit.

A policeman was walking down the High Street when he saw a man with a gorilla on a lead.
'You can't stroll around with a gorilla' said the policeman. 'Take him to the zoo.'
The next day the policeman again met the man and the gorilla in the High Street.
'I thought I told you to take that gorilla to the zoo?' said the policeman. 'I did.' said the man. 'And today I'm taking it to the pictures.'

A man bought two parrots and was told by the petshop owner to keep them apart because one was timid and the other aggressive. But he ignored the advice. The following day, when he took the cover off the cage, the timid parrot had been killed by the aggressive one. To teach it a lesson, he then bought a buzzard. But when he took the cover off the cage the next morning, the parrot had killed that, too.

The man then bought an eagle, but in the morning he took the cover off, and the eagle was dead on the floor of the cage. But this time the parrot was completely bald. There was not a feather on it. It sat naked on its perch, looked up disapprovingly at its owner and said: 'I really had to take my coat off to that one.'

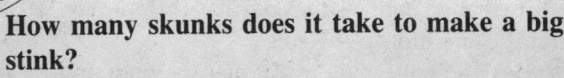

How many skunks does it take to make a big stink?
Quite a phew.

When does a chimpanzee chase a banana?
When the banana splits.

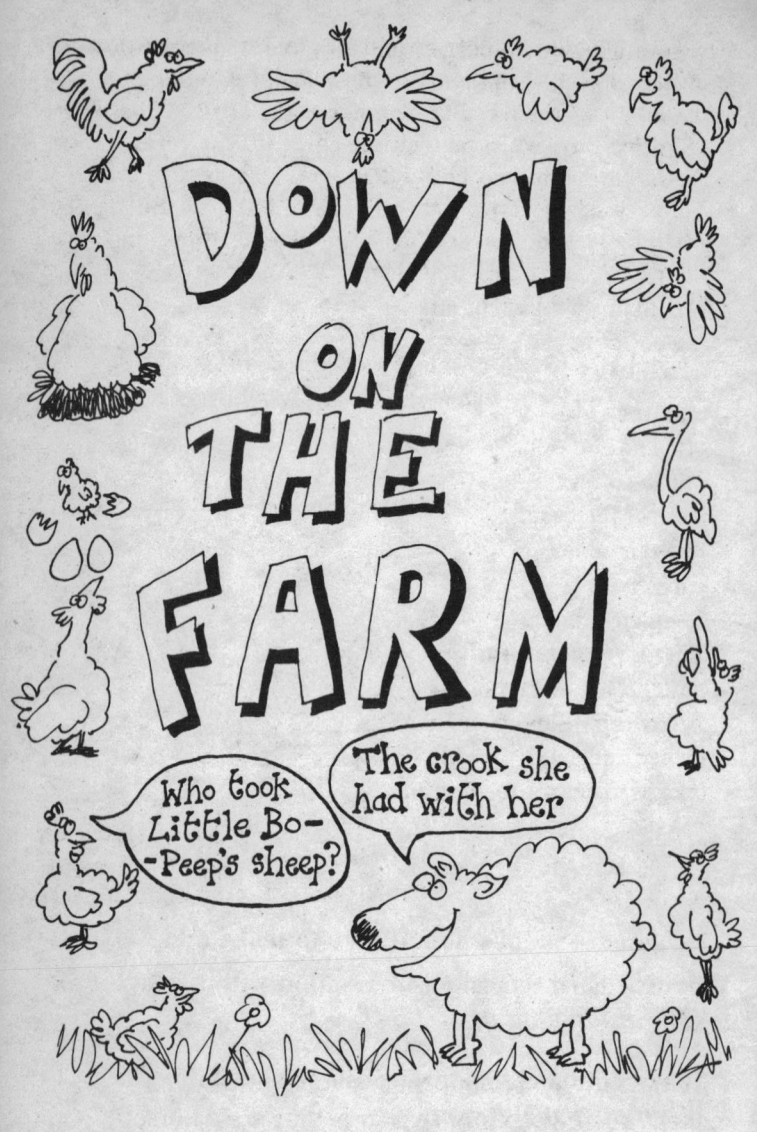

Visitor: 'That farmer's a magician!'
Yokel: 'What, old Farmer Giles? How do you know?'
Visitor: 'He told me he was going to turn his cow into a field.'

What do you call it when pigs do their laundry?
Hogwash.

Why did the Romans build straight roads?
Because they didn't want to drive their horses round the bend.

What is the best way to prevent milk from turning sour?

Why is it hard to make conversation with a goat?
It's always butting in.

City boy: 'Why doesn't that cow have horns?'
Yokel: 'Well, the main reason is that it's a horse.'

Why did the farmer feed his cow money?
He wanted rich milk.

Why did the cow-slip?

'Cos it saw the bull-rush.

Why did the cow jump over the moon?
Because the farmer had cold hands.

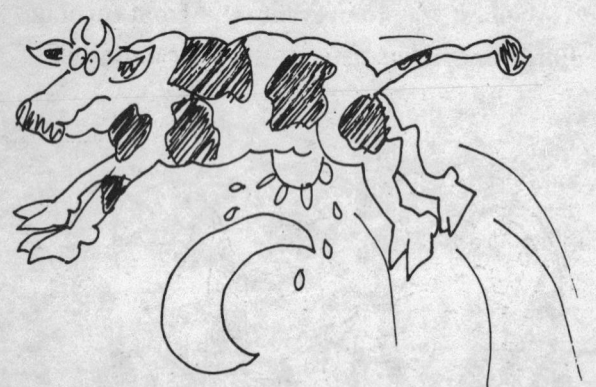

What did the bull say after his visit to the china shop?
'I've just had a smashing time!'

Teacher: 'Name ten things with milk in them.'
Pupil: 'Milkshake, tea, coffee, cocoa and, er . . . six cows.'

If you cross a pig and a young goat, what do you get?
A dirty kid.

How do you take a sick pig to hospital?
In a hambulance.

What is the most important use for cowhide?
Holding the cow together.

What do you get if you cross a cow with an octopus?
An animal that milks itself.

Why didn't the piglets listen to their grandfather?
Because he was an old boar.

Why are bulls so noisy?
Because of their horns.

Why does a baby pig eat so much?
To make a hog of itself.

What did one pig say to the other pig?
'Let's be pen pals.'

What's the difference between a horse trainer and a tailor?
One tends mares; the other mends tears.

Why is wheat like a donkey?
Because they both have long ears.

How do you hire a horse?
Put a brick under each leg.

What is a horse's favourite game?
Stable tennis.

**Why is a horse like
a ball game?**
*Because it gets
stopped by the rein.*

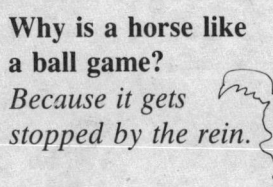

What are assets?
Little donkeys.

**Did you hear about the mad scientist who has
discovered how to make wool out of milk?
It's bound to make cows feel sheepish.**

Roger: 'Mum, do you water a horse when it's thirsty?'
Mother: 'That's right.'
Roger: 'Then I'm going to milk the cat.'

Why aren't horses well dressed?
Because they wear shoes but no socks.

Spell hungry horse in 4 letters.
M T G G.

Did you know it takes three sheep to make a sweater?
I didn't even know they could knit.

Why did the boy stand behind the donkey?

He thought he would get a kick out of it.

What's a horse that left its stable called?
A refugee-gee.

What's made of wood, and swings from branch to branch?
A rocking horse.

Which animal goes to sleep with its shoes on?
A horse.

Why did the water jump?
Because it saw the horse box.

How can you make a slow horse fast?
Don't give him any food.

What's the best butter in the world?
A goat.

Why are goats easy to fool?
Because they swallow anything.

What do you get if you cross a pig with a flea?
Pork scratchings.

What did the bull say when it swallowed the bomb?
Abominabull!

What keeps sheep warm in winter?
Central bleating.

What's hot, greasy, and steals cattle?

A beef burglar.

What do you get if you cross a cow with an Arab?
A milk sheik.

What is a dark horse?
A nightmare.

What's pink and can't stand still?
A pig in a tumble-drier.

What's the difference between a biscuit and a cow?
I don't know. What is the difference?
Have you ever tried dunking a cow in your tea?

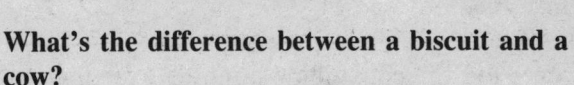

What do you get if you cross a cow, a sheep and a baby goat?
The Milky Baa Kid.

What route did the cow follow jumping over the moon?
She went the Milky Way.

Emma: 'My new horse is very well-mannered.'
Joanne: 'That's nice.'
Emma: 'Not really. Every time we come to a jump, he stops and lets me go first.'

What's a pig's favourite ballet?
Swine Lake.

Why do cows wear bells?
Their horns don't work.

What has five legs and gives milk?
A three-legged cow and a milk-maid.

What do lady sheep wear?
Ewe-niforms.

What's an American cow called?
A Moo Yorker.

What do sheep look for at the sales?
Baagains.

What's black, white, green and brown?
A cow with a runny nose in a muddy field.

What's creamy and good for sick pigs?
Oinkment.

The soccer team were surprised when the new signing turned out to be half-man and half-horse.
'He's our new centaur-forward,' explained the manager.

Why do ducks go out in the rain?
Because they're quackers.

Who took Little Bo-Peep's sheep?
The crook she had with her.

What does a pig use to write his letters with?
Pen and oink.

What lives in the Atlantic and goes 'baaa' at the ships?
A ewe-boat.

Theatre usherette: 'Excuse me, sir, there are two horses in the foyer.'

Manager: 'Two horses? What on earth do they want?'

Usherette: 'Two stalls for Monday night!'

Who led 10,000 pigs up a hill and then back down again?
The Grand Old Duke of Pork.

When is a horse like an artist?
When he draws a cart.

What games do cows like playing?
Moo-sical chairs.

What goes 'clip'?
A one-legged horse.

Why is a pig one of the most unlucky animals in the farmyard?
Because it is killed before it is cured.

What do you get from nervous cows?
Milk shakes.

What do you call a pony with a sore throat?
A little hoarse.

What is a horse's favourite TV programme?
Neigh-bours.

Why was the sheep arrested on the motorway?
Because it made a ewe turn!

What happens if pigs fly?
Bacon goes up.

What's a cow's favourite TV show?
Dr Moo.

What has two heads, one tail, with four legs on one side and two on the other?
A horse being ridden side-saddle.

Where would you find a pre-historic cow?
In a moo-seum.

What animals follow everywhere you go?
Your calves.

How do you shoe a horse?
Say 'Giddy-up!'

What do you call a pig who tells dreary jokes?
A big boar.

What's best for a sick horse?
A visit to the horspital.

What do you get if your sheep studies karate?
A lamb chop.

What happened at the badly organized milking contest?
There was udder chaos.

What did the ram say to his girl-friend?

Where do cows go on a Saturday night?
To the moo-vies.

What do you get if you cross the M1 with a pig?
A road hog.

What do you call a horse with two legs?
Rocky.

How is a pig like a horse?
When a pig is hungry he eats like a horse, and when a horse is hungry he eats like a pig.

Mean Knight Sir Skinflint went into a saddler's and asked for one spur.
'One spur?' said the saddler. 'Surely you mean a pair of spurs, sir?'
'No, just one,' replied the Knight. 'If I can get one side of the horse to go, the other side is bound to come with it!'

What's the best way to count cows?
On a cow-culator.

43

What did one horse say to the other?
I can't remember your mane but your pace is familiar.

What is a buttress?
A female goat.

Why does a horse have six legs?
It has forelegs in front and two behind.

What happens if you walk under a cow?
You get a pat on the head.

How did Mighty Pig explain his success as an actor?
'I ham what I ham.'

What do you get if you cross a porcupine with a mole?
Tunnels that leak.

What did the Daddy Hedgehog say to his son as he was about to spank him?
This is going to hurt me far more than it will you.

What's green and prickly?
A seasick hedgehog.

What did the young porcupine say to the cactus?
'Mummy?'

Why did the hedgehog cross the road?
To see his flat mate.

What sound do two hedgehogs make when they kiss?
'Ouch!'.

How do hedgehogs play leapfrog?
Very carefully.

What do you get if you cross a porcupine and a young goat?
A stuck-up kid.

What do you get when you cross a porcupine with a goat?
A kid that's hard to handle.

Who won the fight between the hedgehog and the fox?
The hedgehog won on points.

**What's got feathers and goes
'C.c.c.c.c.c.c.c.c.c.c.c.c.c.c. . . ?**
A rooster with a bad stutter.

Why did the hens refuse to lay any more eggs?
Because they were tired of working for chicken feed.

What did the Spanish farmer say to his chicken?
'Olé!'

What has two legs, rides a broomstick, goes to the seaside and won't go in the water?
A chicken sand-witch.

Dad: 'For our next Christmas dinner I'm going to cross a chicken with an octopus.'
Mum: 'What on earth for?'
Dad: 'So we can all have a leg each.'

What do you get if you cross a chicken with gunpowder?

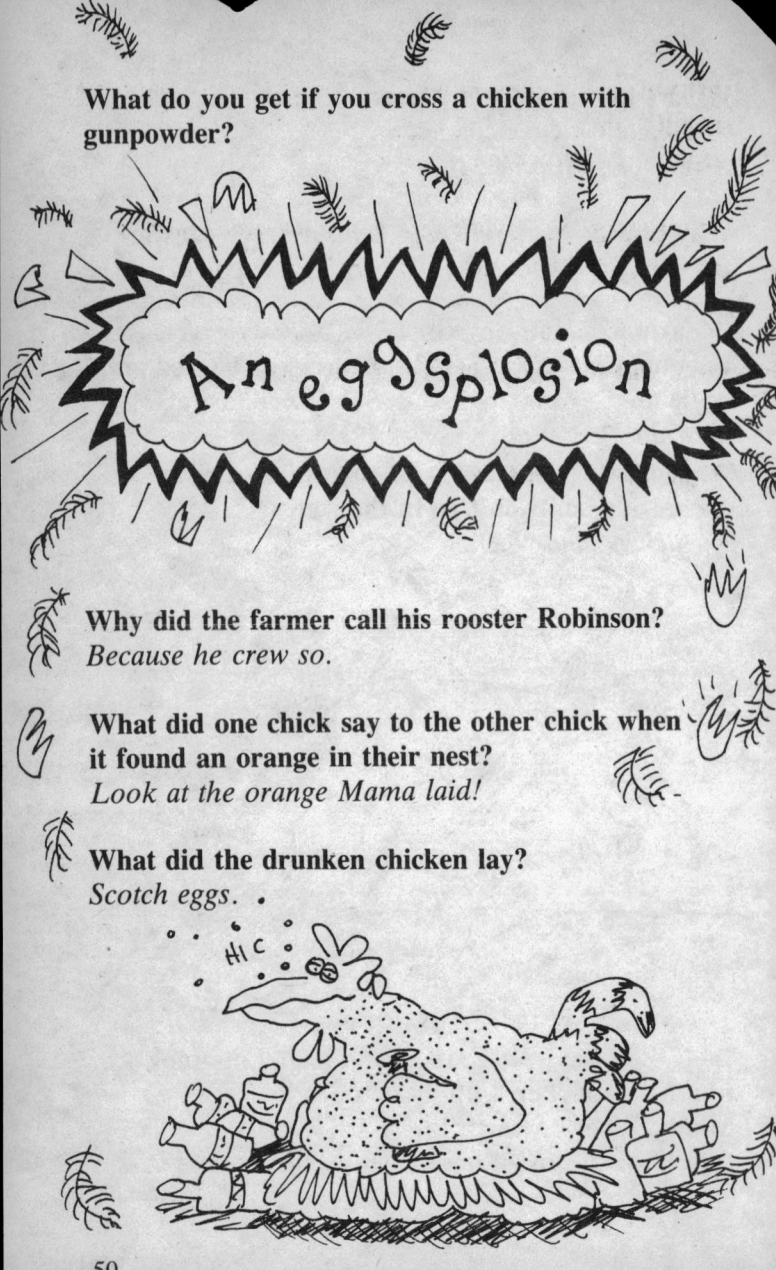

An eggsplosion

Why did the farmer call his rooster Robinson?
Because he crew so.

What did one chick say to the other chick when it found an orange in their nest?
Look at the orange Mama laid!

What did the drunken chicken lay?
Scotch eggs.

HIC

Why would a compliment from a chicken be an insult?
It would be fowl language.

What's a hen's favourite TV programme?
Hatch of the Day.

A farmer hadn't any chickens. Nobody ever gave him any. He never bought, borrowed, begged or stole any. Yet he had an egg for breakfast every morning. How?
He had ducks.

How do hens dance?
Chick to chick.

What's a chicken's favourite cake?
A layer cake.

What do you get if you cross a chicken with a waitress?
Neatly laid eggs.

52

53

What is the opposite of cock-a-doodle-do?
Cock-a-doodle-don't.

What does a poultry farmer drink?
Cocktails.

What do you get if you cross a hen and a guitar?
A chicken that makes music when you pluck it.

Who conquered half the world, laying eggs along the way?
Atilla the Hen!

Why does a lighthouse keeper raise hens?
So that he will have beacon and eggs.

Why can't idiots raise chickens?
They plant the eggs too deep.

What made the chicken run?
It saw the fox trot.

A farmer's daughter, carrying a sack towards the house, says to her friend: 'If you can tell me how many chickens I have in this sack, I'll give you both of them!'

What's covered in feathers and cracks jokes?
A comedi-hen.

What is coq au vin?
A chicken on a lorry.

What do you call a man with a seagull on his head?
Cliff.

Man at auction: 'I've bid a great deal of money for this parrot. Are you sure he talks?'
Auctioneer: ' 'Course I'm sure. He's been bidding against you.'

> Henry spent months teaching his parrot to tell jokes. When the bird was word perfect, Henry took it into his local pub and showed it off.
> 'Pull the other one, Henry,' mocked the regulars.
> 'We'll give you ten-to-one it can't tell a joke.'
> 'Right,' said the man. But try as he might, he couldn't get the bird to utter a sound.
> Outside, Henry cursed the parrot and said 'Why, oh why were you silent, you rotten old bird.'
> The parrot replied: 'Don't be daft. . . Tomorrow you'll get 100-to-one.'

What dance do ducks prefer?
A quackstep.

What's black and white and spins round at 10 miles an hour?
A penguin in a cement-mixer.

'Look how fast he's going' said one eagle to another as a jet hurtled over their heads. 'Hmph,' snorted the other. 'You'd fly fast, too, if your tail was on fire!'

Customer in petshop: 'Why can't you replace my lost canary?'

Petshop owner: 'Because I wouldn't fit into the cage.'

What do you get if you cross a homing pigeon and a woodpecker?

A bird that not only delivers messages, but knocks on the door first.

Why couldn't the pelican get any more groceries on credit?

Because he had too large a bill.

How is a bird on a fence like a coin?
Because it has a head on one side and a tail on the other.

Why did the chicken go just halfway across the road?
She wanted to lay it on the line.

Peter: 'We had my Grannie for Christmas dinner last year.'
Tricia: 'Really? We had turkey!'

What's a cat that has just swallowed a duck?
A duck-filled fatty-puss.

How do ducks dance?
Slow, slow, quack, quack, slow.

Knock-Knock
Who's there?
Toucan.
Toucan who?
Two can play at this game.

What is a polygon?
A dead parrot.

What do you call a constipated budgie?
Chirrup of figs.

What do you stuff a parrot with?

Polyfilla.

How did the exhausted sparrow land safely?
By sparrowchute.

Knock-Knock.
Who's there?
Who.
Who, who?
Sorry, I don't talk to owls.

Why shouldn't you tell secrets to peacocks?
Because they're always spreading tails.

What's a mad blackbird called?
A raven lunatic.

If a man is on top of a monument with a live goose in his arms, what is the quickest way for him to get down?
Pluck the goose.

What duck carries a gun under his wing when he flies?
A hi-quacker!

What bird lives down a coal pit?
A mina bird.

There was a vulture with
a sick expression on its face.
'What's wrong?' asked
another vulture.
'I think I ate
something fresh.'

What do you get if you cross a mina bird with a homing pigeon?
A bird that can ask its way home if it gets lost.

If a waiter carrying a turkey on a platter lets it fall, what three great national calamities occur?
The downfall of Turkey, the breaking up of China, and the overthrow of Greece.

Why is the turkey a fashionable bird?
Because he always appears well-dressed for dinner.

What's brown, quacks and is full of words?
A duck-tionary.

Boy in petshop: 'Have you got any parrot-seed?'
Petshop owner: 'Oh, you've got a parrot, have you?'
Boy: 'No, but I'd like to grow one!'

Did you hear about the man who was prosecuted by the RSPCA?
He bought half a dozen homing pigeons and moved house.

What has feathers and carries water?
An aqua-duck.

If a swan sings a swan song, what does a cygnet sing?
A signature tune.

What kind of doctors do ducks go to?
Quacks.

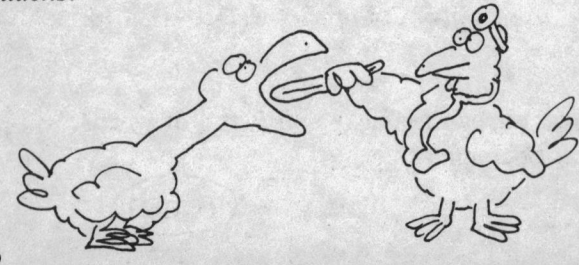

Woman in petshop: 'Can I have a parrot for my son please?'
Petshop owner: 'Sorry, madam, we don't do swops.'

Why should an owl be offended if you called him a pheasant?
You'd be making game of him.

What is the difference between unlawful and illegal?
Unlawful is against the law. Illegal is a sick bird.

Waiter, have you any wild duck?
No sir, but we have a tame one we can irritate for you.

What pie can fly?
A magpie.

Tweet

What do you get if you cross a duck with a cow?
Cream quackers.

What do ducks like on television?
Duckumentaries.

Why are owls brave?
Because they don't give a hoot about anything.

What's Batman doing in the tree?
Looking for Robin's nest.

Why did the pigeon fly over the racetrack?
Because he wanted to have a flutter on the horses.

Why do birds fly south in the winter?
Because its too far to walk.

Jack: 'My teacher does bird imitations.'
Sue: 'Really.'
Jack: 'Yes, she watches me like a hawk.'

What's black, sits in trees, and is highly dangerous?
A crow with a machine-gun.

Why did the one-eyed chicken cross the road?
To get to the Bird's Eye shop.

Why did the owl make everyone laugh?
'Cos he was a hoot!

What fish do pelicans eat?
Anything that fits the bill.

What hawk has no wings?
A tomahawk.

**What's brightly coloured and goes
'Hmmmmmmm-cho, hmmmmmmm-choo'?**
A humming bird with a bad cold.

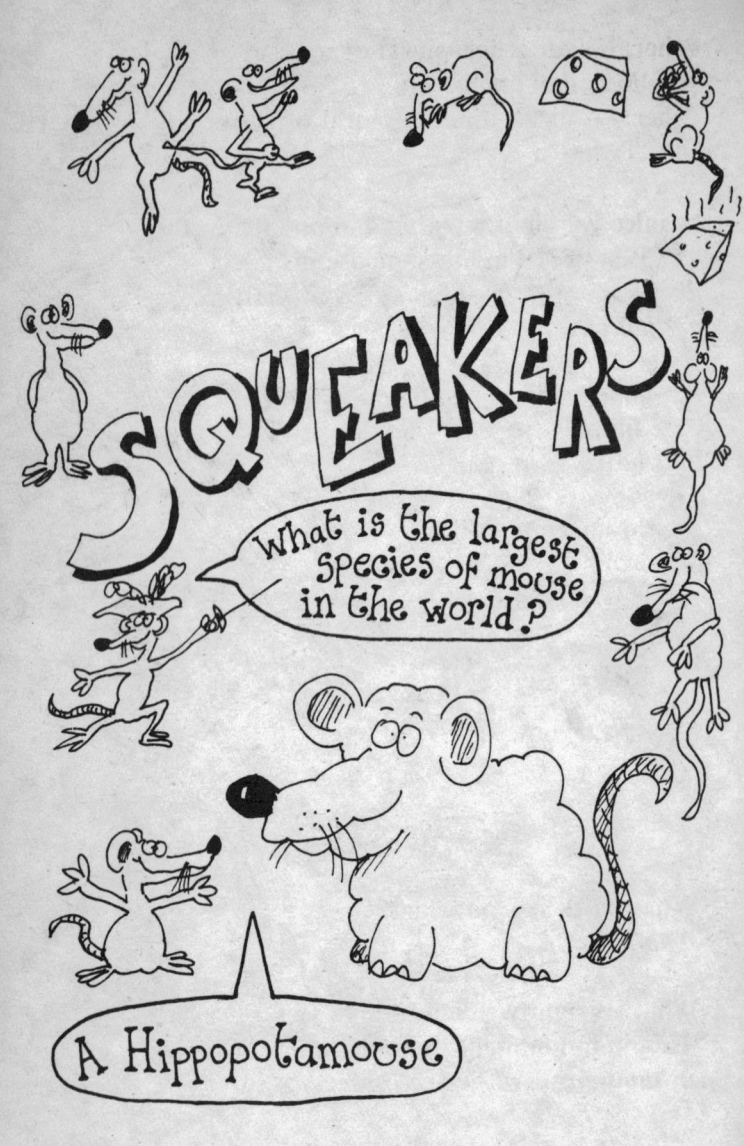

Teacher: 'What is the plural of mouse?'
Pupil: 'Mice.'
Teacher: 'And what is the plural of baby?'
Pupil: 'Twins.'

Two mice were out walking and one fell in the river. What did the other mouse do?
Pulled it out and applied mouse-to-mouse resuscitation.

What happens if you watch too many Mickey Mouse films?
You'll have Disney spells.

What do mice do all day?
Mousework.

Spell mousetrap with three letters.
C-A-T.

What do you get if you cross a mouse and a bar of soap?
Bubble and squeak.

What's grey, buzzes, and eats cheese?
A mouse-quito.

Teacher: 'If I gave you three mice today and four tomorrow, how many would you have?'
Pupil: 'Nine sir.'
Teacher: 'Nine?'
Pupil: 'Yes sir, I've got two mice already.'

A woman rushed into a hardware shop and said: 'Can I have a mousetrap, please? And will you be quick – I've a bus to catch.'
'Sorry, madam,' said the shopkeeper. 'We don't sell them that big!'

Customer: 'I'd like some rat poison.'
Shop owner: 'Sorry, sir, we're out of stock. Try Boots.'
Customer: 'I want to poison them – not kick them to death.'

What's grey, has whiskers and squeaks?
A mouse on roller-skates.

What did the mouse say when he broke his tooth?
Hard cheese.

How do you milk a mouse?
You can't – the bucket won't fit under it.

Why did Mickey Mouse take a trip to outer space?
He wanted to find Pluto.

What has antlers and frightens cats?
Mickey Moose.

What has got twelve legs, one eye and four tails?
Three blind mice and half a kipper.

What's a mouse's favourite game?
Hide and squeak.

What's the worst kind of weather for rats and mice?
When it's raining cats and dogs.

Baby snake: 'Are we poisonous, Mummy?'
Mother snake: 'Yes, dear. Why do you ask?'
Baby snake: ''Cos I've just bitten my tongue!'

Snake-charmer: 'Be careful with that trunk, porter. It contains a ten-foot snake.'
Porter: 'You can't fool me – snakes don't have any feet.'

Why was the baby snake crying?
He'd lost his rattle.

What did the python say to it's victim?
I've got a crush on you.

Why did the viper vipe 'er nose?
Because the adder 'ad 'er handkerchief.

What's hot and tasty and found in the jungle?
Snake and pygmy pie.

What animal has no sense of humour?
A snake, because you can't pull it's leg.

What is long and thin and goes, 'Hith, Hith'?
A snake with a lisp.

What do snake charmers do in the rain?
Turn on their windscreen vipers!

What do you get if you cross a python with a saxophone?
A snake in the brass.

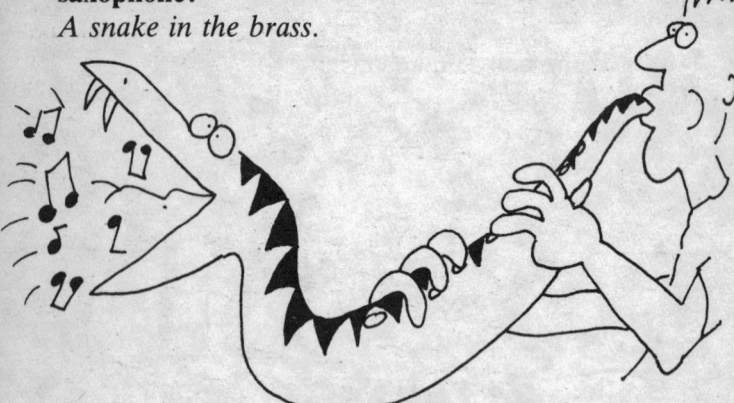

Noah and his wife let all the animals off the Ark when the flood subsided. 'Off you go, monkeys and lions and caterpillars and kangaroos,' he said. 'All of you go forth and multiply.'

Then they cleared up the Ark and sat down for a spot of lunch.

Suddenly, they spotted a pair of snakes hiding in the corner. 'What are you doing still there?' they cried. 'You're supposed to go forth and multiply.'

Meekly, one of the snakes replied, 'I'm so sorry, Mr Noah, but we can't. You see, we're adders. . .'

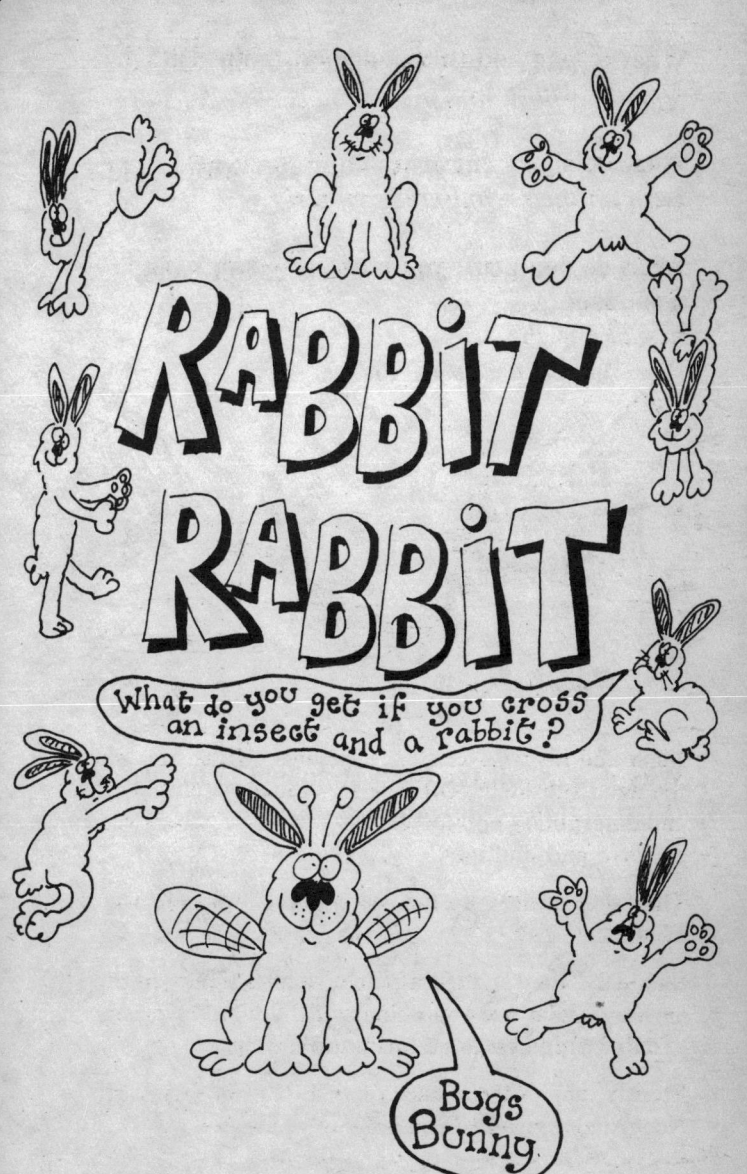

What's the best way to catch a rabbit?
Hide in a bush and make a noise like a lettuce.

What do you get if you cross a hare with a spider?
A harenet.

What has two legs and inspects rabbit-holes.
The burrow surveyor.

How do you post a rabbit?

Hare Mail.

Why is a rabbit the luckiest animal in the world?
Because it has four rabbit's feet.

What do you call a man with three rabbits on his head?
Warren.

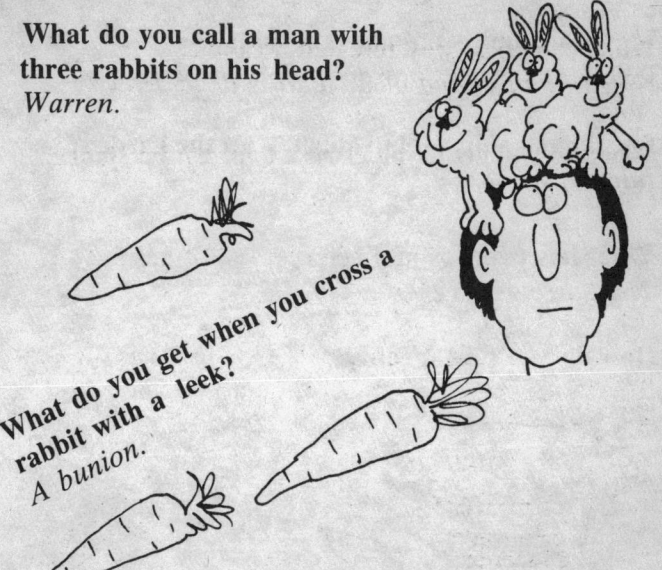

What do you get when you cross a rabbit with a leek?
A bunion.

What is the difference between a counterfeit banknote and a crazy rabbit?
One is bad money, the other is a mad bunny.

Knock – knock,
Who's there?
Rabbit.
Rabbit who?
Rabbit up neatly. It's a present.

Father rabbit to young rabbit: 'Can you keep my daughter in the manner to which she has been accustomed?'
Young rabbit: 'Oh yes, sir. When I marry her, I'll have the doe.'

Why is a rabbit's nose always shiny?
Because it keeps its powder puff at the wrong end.

How do you stop rabbits digging up the garden?
Hide the spade.

Once upon a time, there were three rabbits called,
Foot, Foot-Foot, and Foot-Foot-Foot.
Every morning they would leave their burrow and
cross a dangerous road to reach a field of carrots.
But one day, Foot got run over. The following day,
Foot-Foot said to Foot-Foot-Foot 'We should stay at

home today, in mourning for Foot.'
'We both loved Foot,' replied Foot-Foot-Foot. 'But you
Foot-Foot and I Foot-Foot-Foot must step out into the
big, wide world again because we've got one Foot in
the grave already.'

JUMBO JESTS

What do you get if you cross an elephant with a Kangaroo?
HUGE holes all over Australia

What do you get if you cross an elephant with peanut-butter?
Either peanut-butter that never forgets or an elephant that sticks to the roof of your mouth.

How can you tell if an elephant's been in the fridge?
There'll be giant footprints in the butter.

Why do elephants have trunks?
They'd look silly with suitcases, wouldn't they?

What do you get if you cross an elephant with a canary?
A very messy cage.

How do you know when there's an elephant in your custard?
When it's ever so lumpy.

Who takes longer to get ready for a trip – an elephant or a rooster?
The elephant. He has to pack a trunk while the rooster only takes his comb.

Is it difficult to bury a dead elephant?
Yes, it's a huge undertaking.

What do you get if you cross an elephant with a crow?
Lots of broken telegraph poles.

What do you get if you cross an elephant with a mouse?
Enormous holes in the skirting-board.

Why are elephants grey?
To distinguish them from blackberries.

What's bright blue and weighs 4 tonnes?
An elephant holding its breath.

What's the difference between elephants and fleas?
Elephants can have fleas but fleas can't have elephants.

How do you make an elephant sandwich?
First of all you get a very LARGE loaf. . .

Why do elephant's wear hats?
So they can't be seen in a crowd.

How can you tell the difference between an elephant and a monster?
A monster never remembers.

What's grey and makes you touch the ceiling?
An elephant under your bed.

What's pink, slimy and weighs 5 tonnes?
An inside-out elephant.

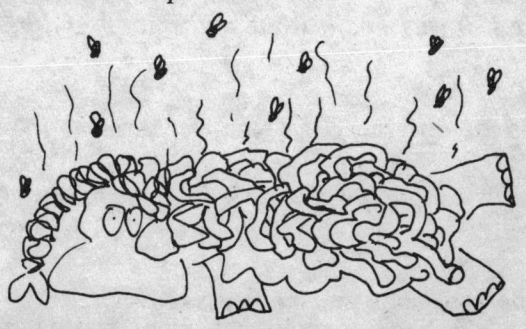

How can you stop an elephant from passing through the eye of a needle?

Tie a knot in his tail.

Why did they throw the elephants out of the swimming pool?
Because they couldn't hold their trunks up.

What's the difference between an Indian elephant and an African elephant?
About five thousand kilometres.

Why is an elephant large, grey and wrinkled?
Because if it was small, white and smooth it'd be an aspirin.

What's big and red and hides its face in the corner?
An embarrassed elephant.

Name nine animals from Africa.
Eight elephants and a giraffe.

How do you get an elephant in a matchbox?
Take out the matches first.

What did the elephants play in the back of the Mini?
Squash.

How can you tell if an elephant's been in your bed?
It'll be full of peanut shells.

Why are elephants so wrinkled?

Just you try and iron one.

'You're late,' said one frog to another.
'Yes,' replied his friend, 'I got stuck in
somebody's throat.'

How did the frog cross the road?
It used the Green Cross Toad.

What's green, and makes a loud noise?
A frog horn.

What do frogs wear in summer?
Open-toad sandals.

What does a frog with bad eyesight do?
Goes to the hoptician.

Did you hear about the unlucky princess?
*She kissed a handsome prince – and he turned
into a frog.*

What sits on a lily-pad and says; 'Cloak, cloak?'
A Chinese flog.

What's a frog's favourite flower?
A croakus.

What's a frog's favourite drink?
Croaka-Cola.

What do frogs fly flags from?
Tadpoles.

The bus conductress was charged with witchcraft. 'Tell me what happened,' said the judge. 'Well, your honour,' she replied, 'when we got to the terminus I said "All Change" and suddenly I had a bus full of frogs.'

What pantomime story is set in a chemist's shop?
Puss in Boots.

Why don't cats shave?
Eight out of ten owners prefer whiskers.

John: 'My cat took the first prize at the Bird Show.'
Freda: 'How did he manage that?'
John: 'He ate the prize canary!'

What's catarrh?
The sound a cat makes when a doctor looks down its throat.

Why did the cat join the Red Cross?
It wanted to be a first aid kit.

Why are alley cats like unskilful surgeons?
Because they mew till late and destroy patience.

What has four legs, a tail, whiskers, and flies?
A dead cat.

How do you get milk from a cat?
Take its saucer away.

Housewife: 'Do you sell cat's meat?'
Shopkeeper: 'Only if they're accompanied by a human being.'

How does a cat feel when he's cleared all the mice out of the house.
Mouse proud.

How do you raise miniature cats?
Feed them on condensed milk.

What do cats prefer for breakfast?
Mice crispies.

snap   crackle   pop

What's the difference between a unicorn and a lettuce?
One is a funny beast, the other is a bunny feast.

What do rich turtles wear?
People-necked sweaters.

Why did the zookeeper run after the lady?
Because she was leaving with a mole on her nose.

In what kind of home do the buffalo roam?
A very dirty one.

Customer: 'Have you any dogs going cheap?'
Petshop owner: 'Sorry, sir, all our dogs go woof.'

Three hunters were trying to identify a pair of tracks.
The first said they must be deer tracks. The second
hunter was sure they were rabbit tracks. Before they
could make up their minds what the tracks were, a
train ran them over.

**Did you hear about the stupid dog who sat down
to gnaw a bone?**
When it got up it only had three legs.

What do you say to a legless dog?
Draggies!

What's brown, has three humps, and lives in the desert?
A camel with a rucksack.

What do animals read in zoos?
Gnus papers!

What's shiny and roars along the sea bed at 100 miles an hour?
A motorpike.

What's 15 metres long and jumps every two seconds?
A dinosaur with hiccups.

What do you call a camel at the North Pole?
Lost.

What animal would you like to be on a cold day?
A little otter.

What do you get if you cross a sheep-dog and a plate of jelly?
Collie-wobbles.

What has feathers, flies and can lift elephants?
A crane.

How do frogs make beer?
Dunno, but they start with hops.

What's long, lives underwater, and likes Latin American music?
A conga eel.

Why do bulldogs have flat faces?
From chasing parked cars.

What did one fish say to the other?
'If you keep your big mouth shut, you won't get caught.'

FOR SALE.

Large dog. House trained. Eats anything. Very fond of children.

Karen: 'I now have 500 bones in my body.'
Father: 'How's that possible?'
Karen: 'I had sardines for lunch.'

What sits at the bottom on the sea and makes you an offer you can't refuse?
The Cod Father.